TRADER

TRADER

POEMS BY

ROBERT MAZZOCCO

ALFRED A. KNOPF NEW YORK 1980

THIS IS A BORZOI BOOK
PUBLISHED BY ALFRED A. KNOPF, INC.

"Trader," "Dead of Night," "Houses," "Autumn," "Years," "Papeete,"
and "All Night" originally appeared in *The New Yorker*.
"Brothers," "Victory," "Gigolo," and "Ceremony" originally
appeared in *The New York Review of Books*. "Fame" and "Doors"
originally appeared in *Antaeus*. "Dreams" originally appeared
in *The Virginia Quarterly Review*. "Vigils" and "Black"
originally appeared in *Harvard Magazine*. "Honolulu" originally
appeared in *The Hawaii Review*.

Library of Congress Cataloging in Publication Data
Mazzocco, Robert. Trader.
I. Title.   PS3563.A995T7   811'.5'4   78–20622
ISBN 0–394–50603–0
ISBN 0–394–73816–0 pbk.

Manufactured in the United States of America
First Edition

FOR STEPHEN SPENDER

CONTENTS

III

IV

~
*This symbol indicates space
between sections of a poem
wherever such spaces are not
apparent due to page breaks.*

I

TRADER

I

There you'll encounter
The headhunters and the hearteaters

There you'll remember
A doctor's hut a copra station

And the gulls faint as a hint of snow
That dot a shallow bay

There in a dream
As you'll run to it your life unrolls

It chills the spine
Brings you home to the body

Even after the valley's past the harvest lost

Or below the azure gulf
The flags of prophets
That chant the light
The animals without emblems
Just the rocks and the flies

The smiles of those whose faces
Save you from the impulse to die

2

There in spring
The maps never alter

In the ashes of evening
The women drift

The men wear nothing
But emerald palm

On a clear hill
The graves of the islanders bleed

Yet ageless
Caught in the feathers and knives at dawn
They'll disappear

You'll not go with them

Among the wet echoes of the coral
The icy footfall of the combers
Half with the hungers half with the ancestors
That speed them apart in diagonal canoes

A bell tingling at a starveling's gate

The "Trout" Quintet on the gramophone

Dwindling they'll persist wandering you'll halt

In the wake of the sun   in the feasts

That are always inland where you are taboo

DEAD OF NIGHT

The air is sultry
And a light rain falls

The oaks are glistening
On a wet pavement

At the end of spring
In the dead of night

And he phones to say
The baby is a boy

A beautiful baby
The delivery was easy

A son born
On the fourth of June

As a rain falls lightly
In the sultry air

At the end of spring
In the dead of night

And he seems happy in a way
You have never heard before

I better get off he laughs
Or I'll say stupid things

Then the weather changes
And the air turns cold

Snow is heavily drifting
On a white pavement

It is almost dawn
The oaks are bare

And you must not tell him
What you both know

That you are the son
Who has just been born

The delivery was bloody
She couldn't stop screaming

On another June
You will be gone

The air is sultry
And a light rain falls

At the end of spring
In the dead of night

You have never been
Nor ever can be so close

BROTHERS

Now you are silent and sitting at a dive
 You have buried your head between your arms
You are hoping to swim away after a foul meal

I am still young and studying at school
 I am dreaming of a siesta open at the throat
Or a painting of paper hearts making mine sleep

Now you are in Florida before a sugar cage
 You are fumbling among whores
While the yellow chirpers couple in the green heat

I am gazing at savannas of charcoal
 Or small villages under everlasting snow
The foam of my cock running over my legs

Now you are walking the deck of the S.S. *Ticonderoga*
 You are returning to battle to recover your smile
The cities of the moon observing an evening at sea

I am moving outward beneath wisteria on the road
 Above I'll follow paths of smoke in the air
Ahead I'll count thorns of steel flecked with blood

Now you are trembling saying goodbye hurrying to the moment
 You are deserting a picnic where the old brood has gathered
You are banging a door grinding an ax in the secret shed

I have grown through you and I have gone from you
 I am lost to you and I am with you in a far country
The intruder you'll murder in a liana of oaths

Here the burnt maps are remembering
   Here the double scars are unrolling
One mouth on another mouth singing a song more ancient than hate

PEOPLE

I didn't want to grow so the weather gave
I refused the rude touch the cat whimpering goodbye
The dog starving at noon the twitch of the genitals

I didn't want to hustle the toy esplanade
Or prowl the alleys or scramble the docks
The old ports where the ships set off at zero

I never saw myself anywhere so broke away
From the scars of the juggler or the costume of fables
The smiles at land's end truthful as hunger

So you say change but I say hasn't that happened

As we turn eye to eye and you hold me
And tell me it doesn't matter really it's a dream
And I mumble yes we're the same

As tomorrow separates our lips and our hair
And we scan the thin line of the locusts in the narrows
And the rooks above the lakes in the clouds

So I plunge to the stony places
I savage at seed too worn ever to be sown
So you follow and hollow my hand and shout for god's sake enough

So I shrug and say yes we want that

But there are the people
They hang in the shadows and they sing of the seasons
Of the lava of autumn or the ashes of winter

As on another day they sang of the forgiveness of spring
Or they are watching the locusts and the rooks
Over the peaks of the city and I am watching

And you are saying oh we're frightened but not completely
You remember a lesson you cry we still have courage
And courage is beauty

But the people stroll among us

They stumble among us smelly and heavy
They knock us about with bats and with fists
They snarl yeah this one yeah that one

And you are stammering maybe but not now
You are kneeling before them begging beneath them *no more*
And I am telling you don't bother

As the people love among us
They were always among us
So the sun spills the moon shrinks the steps stop

HOUSES

It is hard to go back to women

There are brown leaves on the road
The trees are bare

It is a raw December morning

We seem to have just risen
Wetness hangs in the air

Patches of dormant hyacinth
Or ruined forsythia
Look petrified and meek
An old boulder covered with lichen
Like grass peeling in the distance

It is hard to go back to women

In the solitude that survives
The cold   the pews
Of the still lush dark rhododendron
Extend against the terrace
Past white gravel to a field

The sky low the clouds immense

We sit and watch the nuthatch
The small one with the red cap
Its beak golden in the feeder

Others are trembling among
The empty geranium pots

The dangling roots
Like frozen moss
Caught in the compact earth

It is hard to go back to women

    You sort the names I've lost
    The letters I'll never open

There are soft dresses in a closet
And footfalls on a stair

It is a raw December evening

Soon we'll set out
The leaves gone the rooms dust

TOMORROW

We'll have gone together to the mountain
The sun lapping gently among the peaks

We'll be worn as we grasp the summit
And sink heavily to the earth

We'll follow the mistily descending color
The low clouds of gray or of orange

Settling the air
In an umber glow

We'll sit quiet as two people sit quiet
Who'll share the same smile

Who'll create nothing but the past
And nothing but the future to fill it

Who'll learn to live that way
Who'll say they must

Growing stronger in the sheltering spaces of the mountain
Beneath the slow decapitation of the day

Here a few roses
We'll have torn from the steep brier

Here as the distances come nearer
We'll struggle in silence and in shadow

Here finally when we touch in the deep hollow
It'll be dark already

The last pale sloops evaporating on the ocean
The moths of the moon disappearing in the bay

We'll dare not speak
Knowing what there is to remember

We'll dare not wake
Knowing what there was to forget

Asleep so fitfully
Above the wolves prowling the old route

And below the strangers in the snow
Who'll have gone together to the mountain

ESCALES

How alike the altars and mountains are

    The alps of the tropics
    The mariners at shrines

As we stare
What lips shall open or fingers part

Or sensitive as the mimosa
The small pagoda tremble in the air

The future
I desire you were
Because of that
Above my own your self I sought

Those tides of stone no tide can change

    Later gone I'll follow
    A spire a weathervane the pale
    Persistence of flickering homes
    The abandonment of snow
    Among roofs and trees

You at our window
In a miserly light

Beholding cold and unyielding
The downdrift of a single star

Yet after
As the flags lift

Or the bow creaks
If I write
In love eyes are everything

Your real eyes I never saw

For us
Purity wasn't fit to live
It couldn't survive
These voyages alone that are immortal

On which the ghostly curtains set or rise

FAME

It's the year before the past

Days before
The man has cut a finger
The woman's burnt her dress

There's the owl's light
On the still water

A storm brewing in the hill

The year before the crow
In flight to another tale

The year before the moon
Branches of fire
Ablaze on the night river

Far off
The orchestra at the shore
Playing a last waltz

Far off
The bride in a lost boat
The groom beside her

A withered hand a sad smile

Stop them from coming closer

The year before the past

The end and the future

AUTUMN

The moon's coiled in barbed wire now

Old men and boys
Prisoners in ghostly drives

Harvest the great slopes
That have suddenly become news

The long wing
Of the samara's flickering coolly now

The first fruits opening with a dark moan

In those damp palaces our debts mature

The snaky scales
Of the trees entering the sooty vines

The leafy carcass where the night breathes

Women are painting the silences now

Shells being fed to the mouths of guns
Bullets to the rifles and machine guns

Over the road
The rain hymns its dreamless thoughts

Pines white pines yellow pines
Clusters of evergreens peer in all directions now

And below in the still water
Are the mines that wait for a ship's hull

As a lover for the sight of a loved body,

DREAMS

Burning to death in a dream
He watches himself go up in flames
And as he cannot save himself
A scream rises

High as a trumpet in his throat

And if in his dream
There's no color left he's become a ball
Of black fire slowly
Disintegrating in a moonless sky

And always as his ashes

Drift over a familiar town
The ghosts that hobble among themselves
Are without scars
And the bells that toll in the evening tower

Without flags

And if he asks why are you doing
It why are you destroying yourself
He can only say it is my dream
There's nothing to foretell

And the only past one can ever repeat
Is one's dreams

R & R

Under the weather
At Val d'Isère

I pocket the map
And comb the flag

You remember a song
And never sing

I crawl over a hill
And toss a grenade

You down a drink
And never sleep

Nothing's natural
We stare and stare

The peregrine nurses
Wash the glass

The bellmen part
The peacock's tail

There are zebra caves
Mined with orchids

In the bamboo cathedral
There are ghosts we kill

There are enemy fingers
The hibiscus kiss

Nothing's natural
The days go on

From our balcony
We ponder the world

The evening racers
On the statz

The blue antagonists
Above the Alps

If only the patrol
Could start or stop

If only the rivers
Would meet and touch

Nothing's natural
The darkness grows

The generals yawn
And leave the room

The shrinks smile
And turn the page

In the violet air
The warnings soar

Almost we feel
We are just born

Almost we feel
We cannot breathe

Nothing's natural
The ashes fall

At the edge of town
The moon's our own

As we close our eyes
The steps begin

It does no good
We hear our names

The doors of the cars
Spring open like knives

We forget the pain
And the pain arrives

WIDOW

What do you want
From the dead
Let 'em rest in peace
My neighbor says
As she wipes her eyes
And blows her nose
Tells me at the start
Of the Jewish New Year
They came to the cemetery
And dumb with knives
Struck at the monument
A stone of black lace
And his portrait above
Snarled beyond recognition
Oh it hurts . . .

Now the sky darkening
And the moonflower late
Suddenly without pause there's snow . . .

She sits in the subway
And thumbs the newspaper
Wondering if Calcutta's bloody
Egypt's near
If there's another valley
In which to doze
If the TV left on at her apartment
Will keep the prowler away
An old trick . . . but
It's better than nothing

~

Till the Hudson as it last shone
America as it had been hurry by

And she offers
To the purple roses of Belsen
The soot of her heart
To the oranges of Roumania
The cantor singing
The tales of the lost
The horses in autumn
At the Flatiron Building
Munching sweet rolls
In a clear ache of noon
Her daughter in Florida
And her son *god knows*
The days tight in her purse
And the medals with them
If there's a fire she tells me
You know what I'll take

What else is there

As shadows wait
For the light to create them
And the train waits
In its headlong movement
As the apple
Rots on its sill
And the bent chair dreams
Lilac and phlox
Call to each other
Or drift away

In whatever love that's soured
Or evil that once was good
Wearing all her finery
To Staten Island
Afraid of the spics afraid of the spooks
But they're not gonna run me out
Tasting the breath of ashes
The wreath of stars
Past the last stop at the emptying station

ALL HALLOWS

It's the ghost
That sets fire
To a cave so the mirror
Can speak

It's the ghost
That sits in ashes on a floor
To hold a knife
At its throat

It's the ghost
That remembers all
That it's not whatever
Else bleeds

It's the ghost
That's put out perfectly
With cobweb or dew
Lustrous in grief

It's the ghost
That follows only itself
Only the light of the moon
As it glows beneath

The juniper
Tree as it steps
Idly on a dirt lane
As it judges

The roar of a car
Lost under a hill the cries
Of an infant cast
Down a well

It's the ghost
That as it never heals
Always lives as it never dies always
Looks the same

Never looks away
You'll never change we'll say
To the ghost over
And over

As the night
Drills the shore the terns
Leap out of the waves
The harvest fills

Our rooms
And the ghost blooms
The one sentinel that always
Keeps watch

It has nothing
To do it does all
That is necessary it
Is complete

YEARS

They're past us now

And if they'll circle
Distantly in maps

You'll not make out

The stiffening spine
Of sea air

Nor the twitterings that fill them

They're over the ocean now
A whole day of sunlight

Brooding on Arctic fleets

They'll die many of them
A jumble in chorus

Wings that are forever whirling
In a late city . . .

On the terrace the ghosts shrivel

The waiters rust in their places

With such hymns the flocks continue

The slender tails soar aloft
Or drop away in quiet reeds

~

The bathers meanwhile
Saddled with fish enter the wet night . . .

In pursuit
Always in pursuit

They're brown as the dead moon now

Harps of stone   stream of shadow

And in our dream
Recognize their goal as if cliffs were sighted
Before an awakening storm

II

VIGILS

I sit in the sun
And seem to see everything
I've always been

I rise to my knees
Under the monkey pod trees
And close my eyes

I walk past the dust
Till the three valleys halt
And a fourth says PAY HERE

I move further on
Over the broken glass over the snow
On the road over another year

I know I'll never meet
Who I am that the moon will not rot
Nor the house on the hill call

I wait in the small of my fate
Where no one has stood
Tall and gaunt and the hour late

HONOLULU

for Anita Povich

There are quays here
That disappear into the black water
The way the old sailor

Once imagined the world
To split at its farthest point
Lost in the deepest mist . . .

———————

Occasionally the people stroll alone
In moonlight
Bare feet at home in bits of surf

The echoes of black other days
Mingle with the obscure black shapes
Of picnic tables or banyan trees

The outriggers left side by side
On clumps of sand or the surfboards
Kept in strict and measured rows

While the two yachts *SHANGRI-LA*
And *NY NY* seem to grope one another
At a boat basin near the parking lot

———————

In the lobbies of the dream museums
The carpets wear the designs of jonquil
Sun beasts fathomless roots and maps

At an after hours spot in a "ship's bar"
The porthole or the captain's wheel
Recall no suitable refrain or harbor

———————

Yet to resign oneself to what
Is missing or to what is found
Are these the new beginnings

Those galleries of stars that choose
A snowy sky and mountain those spyglasses
Of sleep that meet a distant forest

The three strange figures on a balcony
With the toys piled high in caneback chairs
Or that boy and girl who'll look down now

Past a dim courtyard as an old woman
In plumeria leaves and red chiffon
Waves a farewell and a huge black taxi departs

PAPEETE

When you walk
At night along Papeete harbor
The route of the traffic
Is strangely faint
And on the boulevard above the trees
The haloes of the street lamps
Do not disturb the darkness of the leaves
And the spires of the yachts
That gently rise out of the deep water
Are still and white as the lights
Of the warehouses on the port
That dip and dissolve in the black sea

When you walk
At night along Papeete harbor
The flags appear
Softer than you've ever known
And the sky's ablaze in pendants of stars
That mist and hang through the tenebrous blue
And among the shadows on the yachts
You can make out the wet figures
Smoking or drinking or tossing dice
And each seems to beckon to you
And across the quay you can greet
Tanned and hardened the young runners
As they move swiftly down your path
Then stop and turn and wait for you
And lastly against the dragonflies
That slowly fleck the air you can seek
The faces of *vahines* in the park
Those women who'll lie
On benches in their French sailors' arms

And wonderingly gaze and smile at you
With eyes that might follow
Clear around the world and do

When you walk
At night along Papeete harbor
Though you'll tell yourself
You're much too old and you are
Though you'll say there's no adventure
Left it'll soon be dawn yet it's here

VICTORY

They'll set out
To the small uninhabited island
They'll get there at noon
To last a week a few days
Gathering the pink leaves
Swimming catching fish sleeping
Beneath the palm trees

A night sky full of stars
They'll dream of women
Or make love among themselves

They'll return after
To the other shore
Loading and unloading the cargo boats
Placing the tin crates over the steep wharfs
Bringing a drink to the white man
Idling on the veranda of the one hotel
Or simply disappear as if forever
Deep in the back villages
Among the pigs and roosters
Their naked children and busy wives

    So life will go on
    Between the two islands

Between the dream of return
And the dream of escape
It's a lesson they'll learn
And unlearn year after year
How to choose and not to choose

~

Between the inhabited island
Where the graves of their families
Gleam in dumb heaps
Decorated with bits of stained glass or shells
And the other uninhabited island
Where no roots are sunk
No one's ever born no one ever dies
One comes and goes as one pleases
The other island
That will always call to them
And never own them
The island that has no name
The island of the gods

THE PERFECT LIFE

The gates clang
Or break in the wind
On a soft tropical night

The gates clang
Or break in the wind
And sing of the perfect life

For you'll understand
There are steps that lead
To a shore no one knows

For you'll understand
The frost of the moon the vows
Of the sea can waste the soul

Not the black
Mirrors not the black rainbows
Not the women who'll plunge in the surf

Not the odd
Stars of Tahitian storms
Not the fashionable watering hole

Not the dreams
Of brothers nor the warriors
Who'll turn silent in pale canoes

Only the last
Island you're able to recall
Only the leaves that drift in lonely droves

Only the sailor
Who'll burn the only map
Or stare at the one flag left in port

Where has it gone
Where shall it be
He'll never tell you now

As the gates clang
Or break in the wind
On a soft tropical night

As he sings the song
Of the perfect life as he sings
To himself of the perfect life

As he swims
Away as he breaks all ties
With the soft tropical night

PENDULUMS

Over the water
The bell tolls

Against the bay the sea plunges

        Flooding the air
        With moths of the moon

 Zones open

        As each surfer turns
        And bends his knees

 Stretches to a distant star

Masses of butterflies
In a fluorescent spray

        Ooze past the black night

The glassy
Decimals of the waves the leafy beaks
Of the skerries

Dart in and out
Of white light . . .

        There are graves
        For the flags we cannot follow

        And for the hungers of the soul

~

But none are known

As they ride
They do not stroke in tandem

Each keeps to his own turf

Nothing stable
Yet nothing lost

In the morning
They'll lie together
On the beach in rucksacks

The morning with its broken shells
And bled fish

And gulls above like wild geese

And small crafts
Tethered to the shore

And those that rock on the green foam

GIGOLO

I'll bless my shirt
That wears like iron
And my belly
That's always flat

I'll bless the swift
Smile of my mouth
And the perfect
Girth of my chest

I'll bless the women
Full of wet laughter
And the playboys
Who can't get enough

I'll bless the sun
That tells me its secrets
And the moon that hears
Only my lies

I'll bless the yachts
That sail without banners
And the fingers that remember
How I began

I'll bless the diver
Who brought me the weapons
And the gambler
Who taught me the path

I'll bless the future
Already forgotten
And the mirrors that ask
Are you who I am

I'll bless the old crows
In the churches
And the leafy spinsters
Pouring out of the surf

I'll bless the red dust
Of the hospital
And the club foot
Of the butcher shops

I'll bless the paper kites
Of departure
And the soft drinks
On the sandbar

I'll bless the grottoes
Where the pianos are hiding
And the faces lost
At the edge of a swamp

I'll bless the sailors
Shooting craps on the docks
And the others who curse
The day I was born

I'll bless my sister
At Cuernavaca
And my brother
At Port-au-Spain

I'll bless the garlands
For the sorcerer
And the serpents
That are everywhere

I'll bless the buttocks
That feed me
And my shoulders
That know the way

I'll bless the debts
Of tomorrow
And the final inquisitorial
Look of black

BLACK

There are a black lake
And a golf course on its opposite bank
There are a street lamp
And a palm tree high above a man on a stone bench
There are a night road
Over which the cars pass occasionally
And a house with black doors
Black windows and black steps

In the house
There are no mail and no telephone
Nothing at all
Left to connect the man on the stone bench
To a world that is lost

Yet he feels he'd be happy
If it always were just so
If there would always be a black lake
To glitter faintly
Under its half moon of dust
If there would always be
A golf course and a street lamp
And a palm tree high above a man on a stone bench
If the doors and the windows
Always were just black
And the steps empty
As the cars that pass occasionally
Over the night road

WITCHCRAFT

Il faut que l'herbe pousse et que les enfants meurent

The monotony of the palms
And the linens of dark grains
The sky foraging in a field . . .

As you stood and observed
The cannibals dance
About the spine of an ancient fire
Watched the tigers' teeth
That pierced their ears
Move in a fury to their lips
Braved a glance
At the edge of a trail
And the brief perfectly white
Beat of a stranger's heart . . .

Was it something you came for
That let you come

The thighs opening in sacrifice
A feast of sago or coconut
The captain drunk and reading *Gil Blas*

Then the laughter
Of the crew and the tale
At the shore of why they put the angel
To boil in the pot

It's because maybe you never
Understood the hungers of the island
That beyond the old worry
Of gravestones a carafe of blood
These incantations are necessary

~

Not the ultramarine wars
The mangrove tears
Not the apothecary of painted drums
The dwarfs emerging out of the night canoes
A circle of spears above a harsh roll of surf
Not even the phrase for *long pig*
That meant human meat
The best taste of all . . .

It was years fleet and glistening
A hymn against the volcano

It was denying god breaking the spell
Slowly the knife turning to crystal
The air thickening with tiny grapes

Yet nothing ever unnatural
As in Europe in the cafés the droll mouth
Insisting *cher maître* was the devil
Provincial to a fault

HOROSCOPE

Once again as when a man dies
The roar of water filling up a stream
Boats in the air pianos in the pines
Once again survivors of a scream
Or the scream of survivors in their graves

The banquets of cities
Vistas of snow or rain
These wash over us lengthening the days

Once again

The house left exactly as before
A wife and son and daughter gone
The rot treacherously consuming
The petals of a name

The ghost of the owner
The spirit of the father
Slowly entering the mirror the chair

Once again

To taste a sky one's never seen
Or cross a mountain that's nowhere
Sell one's soul or fool one's luck
But tiger yellow or salmon pink
The voyage crumbles
Or chills to dawn

And age becomes a monument

2

So on these isles
The tales are set
And those who'll want an early start
Must carry them
To the promises of a port
A ruinous valley close to a bay
Where small groups of believers sit
Milky palm or dewy lap
Determining one's destiny

    Ring on ring
    Of roses tightening
    About a throat
    Wild thyme
    Or *pot-au-feu* hung
    On a garden gate

And if you're there
As Mars or Venus lift
You'll not want to ever cry
Nous étions amis autrefois
Then hear your own prayer
Its hunger lost know it is our life

3

Meanwhile drops of rain
Big as fishhooks
Roll on a neighboring shore

Meanwhile the little party
At the cemetery
The pale faces turning left or right

Suddenly the cafés vanish
The gods disband
Emptying the august street

But elsewhere in a flight of sun
The ground bass players disappear
In peacock blouses or string bikinis
As across eternity's jet black floor
The spangled antelopes shoot ahead

It's not exactly a last year
It is exactly why you'll come
To the seven ages the many families
That plunge through the one root
Accepting shelter from a stranger
The cruel smile of the newly born
At home in the home of the cannibal
Where you'll grow strong
Or not grow at all

~

Once again
Echo after echo
On a darkening stair

Once again
Hugging our laughter
In a serpent's tail

III

CEREMONY

They'll only get the future wrong
The arrangement will never fit
The jug of lemonade the animals
In the field the eternity of fog

But walking along past the tennis court
Abel suddenly turns and Cain sees that he's dead
That among yesterday's shadows the parameters
Of bliss they'll always be twin figures
Circling tomorrow's earth

That what never happens and always happens
Are one and the same

And if at twilight in Eden
The gaunt birds are hungering they'll bring nothing back
They'll take nothing away

In these tales
Cain always wonders what Abel feels
Whether the heart's burnt out
Whether it still glows in the perfect chest

But Abel says nothing there's nothing to say

In dour solitude
Cain clings to the albums of frost
The slaughter of stones telling himself I'm nowhere
I survive that even in hell dreams are separate

Sicles of silver
Never alter the dust on a hill . . .

~

At the casino of a small village
Abel places his bets on the shrouded table

As always he's awarded another round

At the edge of a cliff
Emotionless in his car Cain clears his throat
Wondering if finally they might have peace

But Abel is ageless
His tears no release

Bald and alone
Cain jets to Miami deals at the bar
Plunges with another wife
In the harsh surf

And it's almost as if
The roots of quicksilver
Were changing to phlox
The coral of the sun
Deepening with lilies
The first cry far off the funeral unknown
And a plate of raspberries
In childhood awaits them
Beneath the cool berth of an oak . . .

The cities of Cain
In these continual civil wars
Are always the same

~

At the gates of the forest
The wolves lost to the mouths of the rifles
A butcher's flag grazing the harbor
The prophets in the square digging the pits

Only as the fever rises
At the end of the cemetery
He goes over and over the injuries
The injustices of god
In no hurry at last to argue the dawn
The spoilt pastures the stiffening poppies
The one breath left
That could greet his own
The torn face
Cruel yet never more innocent

So again he enters
The welcoming night

The bent grass whispering
It's right it had to be

The woman on the steps
The children in her arms
The old man in disgust
As he curses the ground

And Abel among the drinks and hors d'oeuvres
The scent of dung in the air smiles at his brother
And Cain in heaven moves darkly before him
Under the green mist of the awakening stars

DOORS

Why should it matter to you

I'll enter by one door
You'll leave by another

The door of a cabin
Sealed with snow at the mouth of a creek

The doors of an accordion
You'll say open again and again in our dream

The heart's door in Nietzsche
The door of decision

The moon's door in *Macbeth*
The door of shadows

The door of bread and wine
Once everything's possible

The door of Dante's Hell
Once everything's gone

The door of the cries of the children
The door in *Medea*

The steps to the doors that are endless
As in the parable of Kafka

The door of an asylum
Against which the broken girl rests her brow

The door of the confessional
The poor soul swears by in despair

The doors that are of two minds
They witness everything

The doors that take you from me
And the door that tells us who I am

The rainbows that disappear
In the moiré doors of the sea

The first and final letter
Under the door of our room

The doors of oblivion
That smell of apple

The doors of eternity
That taste of dew

GEMINI

And it's always
As if the stars were set
You come on clumsy
Heavy mysterious
A boat slowly
Being towed to safety
Gun smoke in the air
At the dock

Apart your women
Wilt in the mist

One screams in her pillow
The other trembles
Opening her legs
Gulps down your shadow
As you groan
In the autumn wreck

There are cars that are tasting
The dust of the freeways
There are the ankles of cows
Stippled in dew
There are foxes who've eaten
The sorrows of mirrors

And it's always
At the edges of water
In a late breeze
A gull dips home
I'll hear you call
And enter your past

No nearer my own
Than the one you'll offer
As you throw me the dice
And toss me your cap
Tell me to take
Luck from a stranger
Frown till I win

And it's always
As if the tale
Had never been told
The pool hall at Taos
Your wife in Detroit
The rabbit's foot
Baring its cleft trail
On your chest
The shore leaves
And back alleys
Myself at eighteen
And you at the wheel
Driving on and on
Through the spring rain

And it's always
The fog lengthening over
The winter cities
The odor of gray shirts
And gray dawns
The glitter of towns
At the truckers' cafés
The moon and the ocean
One threatening color

A valley of thistle
I thought
I'd never remember
As the deserts flower
The canyons draw light

And it's always
In a motel that we strip
And the sky is black
You tune up the radio
And split a six-pack
I read to you
From my dog-eared Plato
Our laughter the same
Our summer the same
As the mountain
Lifts its wings
The weather ages our faces
And far off the sea
Drags itself to port
At Gibraltar at Tampico

And it's always
Years after and years alone
A coffin of conifers
In a field of snow
A thumbprint smeared
On an ace of spades
As I touch your tattoo
And you smile and mumble
Too fast don't last
Kid your breath on my mouth

And once more we're there
Once more gone

To haunt your haunt
Be your companion star
Drunk in the daylong night

IV

FLESH

The first time
I made love to a woman
I dreamed that my mother died

It was summer
And at dawn in the mist
There was her face aslant a bank of flowers
With the eyes closed and as if from childhood
The faint pensive smile of remembrance on her lips
And the hair neither gray nor white

It did not
Strike me as strange
What I found nor terrible
To move from the first woman's flesh
To that of the first flesh I had known
Nor for the dream to suggest both
As they met in the death of she who gave me life

I was not sad
And thought such things right or true
I had no guilt as I awoke in my new home
And could feel the scent of flowers still the room
The starlight at rest on the window pane
And watch a world that was over
And a world that had just begun

Then over the gentle face
Of my mother in her bier
I saw *her* face
As I had glimpsed it in the act of love
Startled desperate and serene

The two in union and almost clear
No more the darkness where I hid and lived

The breath of the sleeping woman by my side
And the other woman lost in the dream

2

Often I've thought of what it would be like
The effect of the death of those I love
Often I've imagined the grave of my father
That I'll visit the path I'll share with the future
When all that has gone out of him
Enters me and all that's left
Is spare and questioning the night earth the wet grain
As we stand together
As we stood apart in life
At the four corners of the heart

   Two hands
   That summer on the porch
   On the dark porch listening to Bach
   Two hands that summer that lift
   To the sky then part

There's no way
To keep our lost ones with us
No way to save the first flesh

A mist settles on the flower bed
Catches among the pebbles
At the bottom of a brook
Searches the grove of poplar
And of oak struggles against the luster
Of the sycamore numbers the toys
In the cleft of a ravine brushes the phrase
Of Rilke on the tabletop fills the heart
The frail heart that must spell all that's left
Till what is left is gone is mute
And in its wake seems as if it's never been

3

I know
There are two worlds in the flesh
The one I met when I first entered the other's flesh
And the one without choice or love perfect just pure fate
The flesh out of which I entered life

In the weight of flesh
I could not always find my own
Nor always inhabit the flesh of others
Or the mirror where I beheld my own
Nor the flesh of men where I sought love
I could not rest my head on a woman's breast
Could not believe in anything
Not even the touch they say
That is one's deepest self

In the weight of flesh
I lost my strength
And now between these two memories
How desperately it hovers

How at summer the light rises only to disappear
The hills in darkness lower themselves
And the poplars at dawn grant no repose

4

It is years since the woman and I have met
Years since we first made love
It is years since I dreamed of my mother's death
Yet both live both wait
On different stairs they take their turns
In different houses travel
Against the light and dark as I move apart
From both live apart from all

If I seek solace
It is because I know it is impossible
Impossible to seek a solace that's lost
It is useless to deserve another's death
Useless to desire another's love
The spaces of night the remembered steps
The torn and the whole
Are one and the same the branches of loss
The branches of fullness the sycamore
And summer blood the hunger
That turns us from death to breath and back

ALL NIGHT

All night
I drift apart all night
In these bad times bad hours all night I look at what's to come

All night
The faces suddenly gone the sicknesses drifting past all night
The smiles of the lost adrift in the faceless dark

All night
Nothing to save them nothing left with which to save myself all night
I move toward the same path they travel as we drift apart

All night
Not in light but the deepest flight and mystery all night
The maps accumulate not to be sorted or known but suffered
                                        without release

All night
We discover in night all the traps that seem to fit in which all night
Our past lives fill the future in which the only traps
                                        are what we've been

All night
The sparrows at rest in the trees and the fingers that close the book
                                        all night
Ourselves and others caught on ice floes moving through the dark

All night
Where we go the day cares not the day awaits its new beginnings
                                        all night
The day prepares its survivors feast those who'll synchronize
                                        their watches with the sun

All night
But the night is different the night harbors the desolate all night
The angels at their portholes the gates in the moon that open or shut

All night
In extremity the night offers its one balm having gone so far
                    go one step further all night
As in an instant at the sea's edge the madman leaps and the shapes
                    of night relent

All night
Yet there are those other faces other voices that all night
Rise about us like white poppies as in a fever we drift in and out
                    of the dark

All night
And if through love they'll enter through the deepest betrayal
                    they'll leave yet all night
They return we hear them at our pillows all night the voices
                    that whisper

All night
Of the dark that is the last chance and all the chances missed
                    all night
The voices that say *forgive the unforgivable and you will heal*
                    else nothing lives

All night
In these bad times bad hours as we drift through our sicknesses as
                    all night
The fevers rise about us and sleepless once more all night we dream
                    our passage through the dark

DREAMS

I

The house is a shambles
And the servants are gone

As Mother
Calls from Tampa
Crazy as a loon

Saying
The surf has lost its savor
The pigeons are sour

Saying
I'm there in the mirror
My throat runs to salt

As Father in the garden
Touches the magnolia
The petals float about him
The petals that are bitter
He turns his eyes from you
    Once they were sweet

    The owl sighs in the forest
    The dahlia sniffs at the moon

At night
Mother cries
Gulp it
Swallow it
A wave of water
And it's over

~

But the steps are broken
The lots have been cast

You're on a freighter

A door in the attic
Creaks in the sun

2

Why are the baby whales
Blooming like roses

Why are the tigers
Snapping at the stars

What is Mother doing
Dancing with a sailor

Why does Father's belly
Slump at the wheel

3

Is it rye is it resin
Is it grain is it flour
Is it orange is it apple
Is it nutmeg is it vinegar

Not that

The moment
The sparrow tests the worm
Swart with the color
Of a dead dandelion

Not that

The moment
The elm licks its spine
The hemlocks along the drive
Collect a fork a spoon

Not that

The moment
The woman sits at the table
And stares at the man
The man tears up the letter
And scrapes at his plate

As the hawks fly over
The clouds that are stone

Save me
She shrieks

4

Does the woman have sorrows
She'll buy a new hat
Does the man have enemies
He'll bang down the phone

Mother beneath her veil
Hides the kiss of the sailor
Father biting the papaya
Slops the seeds in a well

   Far off the storm grows
   The rug sings the milk flows

5

In the depths of the jungle
They've been hunting the animal

In the depths of the jungle
Tilting the spaces of night

In the depths of the jungle
Where the sailor is smiling

In the depths of the jungle
As the woman cracks another bottle

In the depths of the jungle
As the man weeps over *Barron's*

In the depths of the jungle
Where the natives are gathering

In the depths of the jungle
Holding aloft the heart of a goat

6

You will not die for them
You will not be born

Father is he lengthening
To judge where you've gone

Mother is she ripening
In a shawl of scent

    Hunger of shadows
    Is it your path

    Ghost in an arbor
    Is it your spirit

Now the woman combing her hair
Over a long stream

Now the man rising to meet her
So our journeys begin

7

There are tongues that condemn
There are gullets that betray

    If it's foul
    Spit it out

    If it's unnatural
    Let it be

As rain fills the valleys
The tips of the mountains

    Mother eats her purse
    Father burns her photo

    With a little laugh
    Both disappear

You move from bazaar to bazaar
One taste one smell everywhere

DEAR THEO

for James Paris

A crazy man's laughing in the fields
Is it god the father I wonder . . .

That yellow house do you remember
Slowly it is turning to stone
A crazy man's in it torturing the heart
But slowly as it bleeds I am born

They dug him up you know
The crazy man   after the funeral
White and black in the searing rain
The doctors hovering on the lawn

Stars and cornflowers on my palette
And candles at noon on my hat . . .
Here at Arles I've grown a bit crazy too
Yet if let be I am home

Long in the tooth all day
Contemplating that one cry
For years   can you not see it
A cloud boat under the moon

Once it's over they'll
Put him away   once youth's over
As a ship in a bottle
A game of chess in a drawer

I caught him the other day
Kneel in the mist then trot down the shore
There are mountains everywhere
He said *but no shrines*

~

If I lose my self
My self does not lose me . . .
Once at Zundert I observed a scarecrow
Climb above the snow then disappear

Though I am not eager to continue the tale
Though I know all that is involved is grace
Or disgrace that *tout est grâce*
Still I am not crazy

Yet I hear the rain as it falls
A pulsebeat on my window and I see
The face of the crazy man asleep on my pillow
And I weep all night in the next room

Dear Theo   the night I say
The night here and there that is day

Robert Mazzocco was born in New York City. He attended Harvard and Columbia and served two years in the armed forces. He has lived in Europe, Africa, the Near East, and, most recently, the South Seas. He is a frequent contributor to *The New York Review of Books* and *The New Yorker,* and is the author of a collection of essays, *Dancing on the Titanic,* to be published in 1980.

A NOTE ON THE TYPE

The text of this book was set in Intertype Garamond, a
modern rendering of the type first cut by Claude Garamond
(1510–1561). Garamond was a pupil of Geoffroy Tory and
is believed to have based his letters on the Venetian models,
although he introduced a number of important differences,
and it is to him we owe the letter that we know as old-style.
He gave to his letters a certain elegance and a feeling of
movement that won for their creator an immediate reputation
and the patronage of Francis I of France.

Composed, printed, and bound by American Book–
Stratford Press, Brattleboro, Vermont, and
Saddle Brook, New Jersey.

Designed by Judith Henry.